The Planet Of The Immortals

Mehrangiz Rassapour

Bridge translator: Alireza Abiz
Editor: Catherine Davidson

Dedicated to George and Heath McCarthy

With this book, I bow down with all my heart and soul to my precious, beautiful, two grandchildren George and Heath McCarthy. George left us at the age of 14! He was not given enough time to bring his gifts, talents and creativity to the wider world but, to those he touched, he is and always will be an influence and inspiration.

Hidden from sight, he lives on shining in our souls forever.

CONTENTS

I would like to thank all who helped me to prepare this book. Special thanks to Catherine Davidson the editor of this book for her patience and indispensable guidance.

I would like to express my gratitude to my beloved son Ash Rahmat for his sincere and poetic help and support.

Thank you to Ranald Barnicot, my former English language teacher, for his translation of the short poems 'The Stagnant Water' and 'Let's Sit in Homage'.

Also, many thanks to all editors of Persian literary and cultural magazines that have published so many of my poems and of course thanks to *Agenda: Translation As Metamorphosis*, and *Fire* magazines for publishing my poems.

Foreword

Mehrangiz Rassapour (M. Pegah) is a master poet, literary critic and editor. Editing Pegah's poems has been one of the most interesting and fulfilling poetic projects of my career. It has made me think deeply about the nature of voice, and what it means to hear another writer sing in tones that are wholly of another tongue – in resonant English.

The poems in this collection are the work of an intense collaboration in the editing process. Early drafts of some of the poems received translations from Alireza Abiz. Pegah also did her own translations. We then spent a lot of time discussing, debating, sifting, selecting just the right word to bring the Farsi image as close as possible, and the right way to shape the poems to Pegah's unique voice.

The poems are original and complex – in imagery, theme, voice and use of space. In paying such close attention to the poems, I became intimate with a language I could not speak. It was like watching a shadow from far away come closer and closer, until each poem was right in front of us, alive and fully itself.

Catherine Temma Davidson

The Planet Of The Immortals

My spaceship speaks the truth
"Earth is not a proper dwelling
Earth is a huge, decked-out zero"

All that has passed
                        was playful misery
Like concurring while falling
Or laughing while vomiting
Or kissing while coughing

Our presence on earth
Was an irrelevant joke
Like the poet's irrelevance
                        to military ammunition

On earth
Only diseases... have a purpose
And only the dead
                        are all homeowners
And only the skeletons
                        are all smiling

Earth
The earth that like cancer
                        pretends to be stupid!
All of us
Offspring of hereditary intercourse

Constantly...
                conquering deception

We believed our screams
Could make us immune
                to earthquakes and storms
And only our corpses
                made us identical!
We were buried in accordance with a sick law

On earth
God was being tortured
                under the cloak of religion!

Look!
Without any wind,
Trees tremble with such confidence
As if they are precisely scared
"Yes
They are scared, precisely"!

Now
I invite you on a journey
You've been waiting a lifetime
                to dream about it!
This journey
Is an eternal exemption... from bewilderment

Dear Companions!
Please wear special glasses made of
"Another Understanding"

These glasses
                simplify formulas
Using these glasses
Is like eating forbidden fruit
So, you hot tempered earthly angels
                                Be on your guard!

Attention! Attention!
What was called *love* on earth
At the end of this journey,
                is our host

Attention! Attention!
What was called *body* on earth
Is not with us on this journey

The body was a seed
Sown on the earth
                to scatter us
The body was a sign of the existence of distance!

Now you can see through your glasses
A fascinating war
                between your memories
                has broken out
                and they have all surrendered!

That star luxuriating in glitter
Is a planet where
                our arrival is being celebrated
And that vanishing spot

Is the earth
surrendering to an engulfing law

Now a pleasurable fear
captures our feelings
And we are going to be dissolved
In the radiance of perception
And a new human being
a new symbol
Steps on the "Planet of the Immortals"

A woman brought you to the Earth!
And a woman took you from the Earth!

Liar Soil

Yes...
from Earth,
I remember only

> its innocent beetles
> the fakery of its blues
> the clown seasons
> ridiculous birds
> stupid living waters
> enormous garbage bags
> pitiful windows
> and miserable humans

On Earth
Only religions
> were godless!

Now, I walk the streets of Mars
The soil is pink
The sky is pink
> and I am awaiting the dawn
> to see the crimson morning too

(I don't know what to expect from a star.)

I stare at my earthly body
A heart that will turn to dust
A brain that will turn to dust
Disgusted at these hollow bones
No eyes
> No brain
> > No tongue

Just bone
Just cavity, just teeth
An ominous end! An ominous end!

Respected citizens of Mars!
I'm a handful of soil from the Earth
Arrived on your planet by foot
                              to see your pink sky
Currently
        on Earth, dance contests
        and car racing are underway

"Liar soil! Liar soil!
Currently wars are being fought on Earth
                                    over God!
Liar soil!
You have polluted the blue,
Polluted the green,
And now have come to pollute the pink too."

Respectful residents of Mars!
I am a handful of soil from the Earth
I've brought lies to your planet
If I blindfold the sun one day
And say
Everyone is happy on Earth
Will the sun believe me?

How many degrees below zero truth
                          should I go... then?

Another Type Of Suicide

What a withered and hollow sky!
"Humanity is earth's masterpiece?"
Ha-ha!
         What creased, wrinkled words!
My mother's womb
Was more flourishing than this world

I folded life
And put it in my bag
         saying: sorry God!
I acted like someone hopeful and alive
Shook hands with anticipating incidents
And through circumspect walls,
         ...I passed

And like a lion
Surprised by an armed baby
I made the world surrender!
         "Hands up!
         Empty Your Pockets!"

Hollow medals of heroism
Fame without ownership
Fetid mornings of whorehouses
Ridiculous faces of religion
         under the soot of lies
Queues of terrified prophets
         apologizing to people
Academic lusts of sterile scientists
Forced freedom of waves

Faithful torturers
Shredded protests
Mouldy jobs
Shining historical defeats
Unfinished chattering
Travelogues of internet tourists
Screech of ideological mobiles
Squawking of postmodern poets
Scattered cigarette butts
    surrounding the thoughts of failed new-borns
Holy books, intercourse, toilet, condom,
Empty bottle, famine, bullet, vulture...
       and blood
Blood spouting
   from the pores of its pockets.
   "Puke!"

The world passed out from the truth of my nausea
And I burst into laughter
    at the impact of my nausea
Ridiculous unconsciousness!

"Death to a world too weak
    to overcome a smirk
Worthy of the paltry rebellions of a coward."
Now here you are
   corpse of the world!

It was obvious from when I was a sperm
    I would be suicidal!

Short Poems

Be like water
Even if you avoid passing through flowers and grass
Grass and flowers grow...

      from wherever you pass!

* * *

You're a scientist... I am a poet
I understand the flower, intact,
But you, to understand,
You tear it into pieces... with your hands!

* * *

Let's sit in homage
To the heroism of flowers
     Still growing!

* * *

I am that refractory fish
That has escaped
In the mouth of an eagle
     to the sky!

* * *

The stagnant water
Is docile, moulded to the bowl's shape
But the flowing water
    takes the bowl with it!

All The Lost Are Alike

But you!
Have embedded frightening kisses
                              in your kindness
And have dug trenches in the fortress of your smile!

You want to interpret your nightmares
                              through fictional events
And you deprive me of the sky
As if
        the sky were inherited from your ancestors!

I know
Thirsty,
You'll run mistakenly towards your lover's address
And in the desert
                  you will be prey to a mirage…
Then you'll scream:
                  "All the lost are alike!"
May your screams be met by my laughter!

No road is responsible for comings and goings.

From The Big Bang Till You

Although this city is good food for an earthquake
Don't worry!
The earthquake has targeted only... my home!

It's obvious from its hesitant, trembling uproar
It is sailing
       in the stormy mirage of its own stupidity

With its illusion
Which has taken refuge in delusion,
It wants a favourable return on its desire
For my astute truth
          Ha ha...

I!
Who have been desired by all the lovers in the world!
In swift heated lovemaking
From the Big Bang... till you!

I was a zygote
When this love was assigned to me
Otherwise, I never wanted to be born
In a temporary body
On a buoyant planet in space.

I was not going to be a cosmic creature
Among those
Who crush or cook each other

They fall in love at first sight
And scare each other
                at the second glance!

Those who roll over each other...tightly
                                in the dark
And in the light,
Under the sweat of their escape velocity
                        rinse out their regrets
With non-stop complaints.
They have competed
With greedy, unbalanced scales
And charge each other
The cost of their heart-wrenching sympathies
With their fearful bluffing!

They are sociologists...who do not know themselves.
They practice kissing
                but prefer biting!
And from their stone-glass eyes
                they weigh each other's genitals.

The whole aim of my birth was to see you
Otherwise, I was not the kind of person to play in hell

I!
At the multiplicity of your excellence
My memory faints
So that I forget
The ocean is swimming

In the tears of my amazement!

Feeling helpless in praising you,
I claw at the ground
And a phenomenal spring flows
                    from under my nails
All the flowers in the world
Want to smell its fragrance
And insist on growing... beside it
A spring so glittering
The sun lays prostrate before it!

Although all of you
Would serve as good corpses for an earthquake
Don't worry!
That earthquake has come just for me!

It has come to desiccate
The root of love's fertility
                    in my consciousness
It doesn't know that
Its dream will be shattered
So completely only a hurricane
                    could stick its particles back together!

Don't be afraid!
Fear turns darkness opulent

With a special sigh
I ignited the open mouths of the astonished

Then all together
        we sang a fiery song:
"Love's a grain of wheat
Flying out from an electric mill
To feed the world!"

I am a new spectator
Watching me
Astonishes actors on stage

At a house
Where the sun hangs itself on the doorstep
                just to see you
It's natural for a storm to become a genius
of its own denial
And for the earthquake
        to get so lost and confused
That it asks me directions to its grave!

But you!
In your hells
Looking for love
        Be afraid!
I am your earthquake...

Contrary to conventional promises
I have come to make hell floriferous!

Love is the metamorphosis of a locker into space

The Ten Year Old Bride

Forced into her starry dress
It was as if they had shaken the night
                              over her
And her murky tears
Suppurating from fear's sores

In a tribe with its mummified laughter
And quadruped hoof prints
On their sludge of imagination

The ten-year-old bride
                    ten-year-old child
They drag
        drag... drag her
                    to her husband's stronghold

Do you want your doll?
                    Your doll died!
Last night
Fairy tale giants
Mounted an assault
Murdered your father
Abducted your mother
Devoured your playmates
And your doll?
          Crushed underfoot
                    ...died!

But isn't she the ludicrous lineage of her mother?

A long wearisome chapter
An agonising likeness
                    taking refuge in her inner turmoil?

The bludgeon of inherited mores
                        on her head
The bludgeon of inherited fear and superstition
                        on her head
The bludgeon of inherited silence
                        on her head

Her today is buried
                    under yesterday's debris

And maturity?
Like the throes of ancient marshes!

Where should she sleep?
                    to set her fearless dream... free

She felt
Her breath withering the flowers
"I'm asleep
            it's a nightmare!
I'm asleep
            it's a nightmare!
                        tomorrow..."

Tomorrow?!
Tomorrow's dawn
                pitch black

The city turned upside down
Your father is an ogre
Your mother is a vampire
Your husband?

       He is the demon of fairy tales!

And the dust
engulfed her so that
no one could see
the wind blowing her

       ...away

Fever And Chills

Fever in the night
Fever in the night
I blow moments up
Blow moments up
           one by one!

I live in a pot
My roots are cramped
My veins arid
My soul confused
My dream a drought
Barren... my infrastructure!

I am the guest of an animal
My water stingy
My bread vile
My earth and sky despicable
Rotten...
       Is my host!

I am the lock of a prison
Ashamed of the door
Ashamed of the window
Ashamed of the bird
Key!
     Come rescue me!

Snow... snow... snow...
Don't take me naked, under the snow
Don't tie my hair to icicles
Ah... my sky
　　　　buried under snow!

Dragon!
Come! With that blazing mouth...
Fire is good for snow!
I'm cold
My bones
　　　　covered in hoar frost!

I am in primary school
　　　　　　　in the essay class

Topic: hell
Pen = matches
Ink = petrol
Class monitor? = Me!
(as if someone said: "light the match!")

I burnt
　　　my teacher burnt
　　　my classmates burnt

Ah... my school burnt!

Woman's Miracle

Desert...
     and the incendiary sun...
But,
     woman's tongue is moist

She licks the thorn's dream
Blossoms sprout on the tip of its claws

She licks the soil's dream
               a fountain emerges

She licks the stone's dream
               it bears fruit

She licks the dream of the driest leaf,
                  taken by the wind
It jumps back on the bough

And woman?
Dances in heaven!

How Good To Be A Woman

I swear by the mighty morning
I swear by discerning hearts
I swear by the final human glance
That these words are the truth
And the truth
                  is in these words

When the stars become eyes
And the earth turns wholly into skin
And the moon screams
And the sun bathes its body, triumphantly

How good...

When the bed
                  becomes men's pride
The bedsheet ripples stormy white
And everything speaks of a pure white clarity
The canary... sings white
The leaf falls white
The wind blows white
The snake turns its sting white
And the woman's skin glows
                  from inner heat
How good...

When the ceiling stares at the bed, thoughtfully:
"There is no honour
In being a ceiling... doomed to dry"

When pleasure

   spreads in its sacred breadth

And stars all turn green

And the sky

   dresses in navy silk,

   yearning for the red moon

And autumn, blue

    moves out of orbit

How good...

The triangles of pleasure

Are measured by a tall subject

Acute angles

Form geometrical lines... venerated

And shadow breaks open

    from illumination!

How good...

A lucky star is a lie

A lucky star is a cursed joy

Let's call lucky violet

Which is gold

   and purple too!

How good to be a woman

When the woman

   speaks golden and purple too!

How good to be a woman

When the woman

conquers the pen

And time pulls itself back
                    on both sides,
                    to open the way for love
And the angel of inspiration
                    begs the horizon
                    "Let me go and come back anew"

And love opens the quotation mark:
"The capacity of a dot
Cannot be more than a dot
                    Little ones!
Zero does not rise
                    Little ones!
You hasty poets!
You Poets pouring tears in a rush
Take pictures with your fame, as keepsake
Your fame is sterile."
And Bang! closes the quotation mark!

The woman takes prophets to bed... openly!

How good to be a woman
when the east, sun in its arms
                    look at the west wisely
And the woman
With divine bravery
                    rises
                    separates... from the earth
Caresses her radiant skin
And under the sternum of her power
                    She feels

        palpitations of rich fertilization
And pleasure's froth
Spills out of her skin's pores
               and she sings:
"The crossing point is Woman
The power switch is Woman
The door latch is Woman
Wave is Woman
Earth is Woman
See how she gives birth
             gives birth... birth... birth
Inhales love
And creates the best line of her ghazal:
              "Human"
Human is the king of the sonnet of the soil!

Don't let happiness drop from that bough
Holy temptations!
Have you glued stars on your heads?

Hey Sun!
Darkness has covered its name with spangles

Grass! Grass!
What silky coquetry... for the breeze!

Dance circulates in your waist
Dance then! Butterfly!

How good
How good
How good... to be a woman!

You Don't Know Me, Bird!

Bird!
      Go
            Go
                 before I say something!

The sky is my space

Someone there
        has scattered stars for me

What have you got?
             Seeds!
Where?
      On Earth!

You see!
Bird! You don't know me!

Every Dawn

Every dawn
       I drank the essence of light

Every dawn
       I laughed at the lifespan of stars

Every dawn...
The cord of your truth
Became a column of light
I climbed up it
        stood
            and understood!

Every dawn...
You sat on the horizon
Like the angel of revelation
(Don't say no, I saw you!)

Every dawn,
       I became the reason
       for night's suicide!

EDITOR

Catherine Temma Davidson is a novelist, poet and essayist who grew up in California and now lives in the UK. Her first

novel, *The Priest Fainted*, was chosen as a notable book of the year by both the *The New York Times* and *The LA Times*. In 2018, she published *The Orchard*, a short novel about family, genocide and apricot jam. She teaches Creative Writing at Regent's University in London.

Cover photo: The Great Andromeda Galaxy, CajunAstro, CC by 2.0
Author photo: Bulent

Design: Jill Tipping
Series Editor: Aviva Dautch
Project Manager: David Clark
EWI Director: Jennifer Langer

MEHRANGIZ RASSAPOUR
(M. Pegah), poet, literary critic and
editor of *Vajeh* (Word) magazine, was
born in the South West of Iran
(Khoram-Abad). She started writing
poetry when she was nine and had her
first ghazal published at the age of 13.
She has published four collections of
poetry, including *The Spark Die At
Once*, *And Then the Sun*, *Birds Are Out
Of Date*, and *The Planet Of Pause*. Her
fifth book will be published soon.

   Her work has been translated into
many languages including English,
French, German, Polish and Italian,
and she has been critically acclaimed
for her powerful and unique voice in
translation and in the original. At the
international poetry festival in France,
her poems were highly acclaimed
and she was given the title "The
Dawn of Literature" in the Culture
section of *Le Temps*.

9781913992095

ISBN 978-1-913992-09-5

These Two Roses

SANA NASSARI

exiled writers ink

Published by Exiled Writers Ink, 2021

exiled writers ink
——————— voices in a strange land

Exiled Writers Ink
www.exiledwriters.co.uk

Working to promote the creative
expression of refugees and migrants,
to encourage cross-cultural dialogue
and to challenge human rights abuses
through literary activism.

Established in 2000
Registered charity no: 1097497

Funded by

Supported using public funding by
ARTS COUNCIL
ENGLAND

Garfield Weston
FOUNDATION

Nina and Roger Stewart Charitable Trust